DARK BIRD

Copyright © Sam Schmidt 2024

ISBN 978-0-913123-43-0

First published by Galileo Books in 2024

FREEGALILEO.COM

Tree photos by the author

Book design by Adam Robinson

DARK

SAM SCHMIDT

Galileo Books
AIKEN, SOUTH CAROLINA

BIRD

Some of these poems, often in different versions, have been published in the following journals, to whose editors grateful acknowledgement is made: The *Free State Review, Passager,* and the *Loch Raven Review*. The poem that begins "Don't pretend you're blossoming if you're not…" is indebted to a column from Knox News by Durant Ashmore, "Grab your chainsaw and end this Bradford Pear curse once and for all," accessible at HTTPS://BIT.LY/KNOX-NEWS.

This book had a long gestation with generous support. From Barrett Warner of Galileo Press who believed in it and made important suggestions. From other poets whose work I admire—Edgar Silex, Clarinda Harriss, and Gregg Mosson—who read the manuscript at different stages, providing feedback and encouragement. From my poetry workshop group—including Sherry Morrow and my wife Virginia Crawford—who showed patience when I brought the same poem back repeatedly. From Virginia, particularly, whom I would ambush daily with questions about word choice and line breaks. This work began as a series of Meta posts. I don't think I could have persisted without reactions and comments from my Facebook community, too many to acknowledge all by name. I would single out Dorothy Dodge, Debbie Ingamells, Llewelyn Lewis, Megg Magee, Rosemary Talia Raun, and Marie Nash Schmidt. Thank you for your thumbs up, hearts, and comments. I also acknowledge the State of Maryland for its 2022 Individual Artist Grant awarded through the Maryland State Arts Council.

for my family

Then a tree. An ordinary tree.
There was nothing left.

A tree revolves among faces.
When I open my eyes, it's back as it was.
It was never a god in disguise.
It won't reveal
a passage through. An exit out.
It's not a young woman—or
an old one—transformed.
Each day, I take a picture.
There's an art to remaining still.
A dusting of snow overnight.
The tree does nothing.
When I close my eyes, darkness.
Here's winter daybreak turning it
from a silhouette into all its dimensions.
Tree I pass each morning with our dog.
In the cemetery across from our house.

That the tree stays the same—
this disturbs me.
My daughter nods.
I would like it to speak
telepathically. Do a tantric
yoga routine. Its bark
is a deep gray not quite smooth.
A metallic sheen.
Horizontal seams.
As if it could peel back in strips.
Fractal splashes of lichen.
At the tips of its branches,
in the twilight: tiny fists.

A distant cry,
full of talons and fire.
Neither part of this world nor apart.
The mind perceives its chains.
Take my staff, a wise woman says.
Walk into the graveyard at sunrise.
Seek out the tree that is many trees,
one beyond the other. Each, a gate.
First, the gate of boredom.
You should pass that without difficulty.
Second, the gate of doubt.
Strike the gate with the staff. It will sound
like a gong. The sun will tremble.
All your sleeping demons will open their eyes.
Every playground bully.
Every peevish professor.
Only they can let you through.
Be brave. Be humble. Remember,
you have heard the dragon.

Snow touches the world.

Draws a thin line along the top of each branch.

The landscape is expectant.

The great toddler god of the cold,

who does not care

about cars getting where they need to go,

rises up with his enormous white crayon.

The snow's too deep. I can't get out

to take the picture, to write a few words.

I'll go out for you, my daughter says.

I took my pictures from one side. She

takes hers from the other.

I was starting to like my unbroken sameness.

After a pause: a white

blissed-out feeling. A vision

of heaven in her small kindness. Heaven,

to one side of the tree.

To one side of wherever I look.

The tree is back to being bare.
More bare than before.
As if at a beginning:
Black against the white.
Wind scouring it clean.
Everywhere the sound of dripping.
The dark things, asphalt, bark,
soak up heat from the frigid light.
The snow makes a faint
high-pitched sound. Melts
against the fugitive warmth.
The solid, the formed, surrenders,
like in love, to its liquid nature.
Drip drip drip. Drip drip drip.
Freshets of water rush through grates into sewers.
The edge of the snow, irregular
like coastlines on charts.
The muddy grass.
A fox trots by.

Daybreak,
like colors for a living room.
At a Jersey beach house.
Walls cloud gray. Trim, a pitch
just shy of black. Peach accents like
the trailing ends
of *la madrugada*
You want the world to be an interior.
It's outside. You will never
get to the end of it.
The sun is more than a ceiling lamp.
It's an unauthorized
nuclear conflagration. In space.
Snow melts swiftly at a low spot in the road,
a tiny terrifying current.
The fox is bounding down
the curvature of the earth.

As if she looks back.
The spiral of her trunk,
a swerving hip, a level gaze.
Her slick sheen, as if packed with feeling.
The wordless sky, eloquent.
The tree is spiky and fierce.
How did I never notice?
A bouquet of talons.
Unopened buds.
Razor-sharp spurs.
Unopened birds.
She stands at the beginning
of a fairytale. Her shape
begins to loom.
Her edges sharpen.
She's a hungry spirit.
A wind upwelling beyond the pines:
About to buffet me. About
to fling me into the sky.
Flat chimes. Slack halyards
beat time against flagpoles.
Flags flapping. The tree thrashing.

Beyond the cawing, the cold: Something
you can't hear is not quite silence.
Tracks through the snow. Footprints and paw prints.
The mercury drops till even the wind freezes.
The land lapses into stillness, odorless, as if
it's a gelatin silver photo.
All the surfaces that gave to the touch
are hard. Even ridges of mud
where a hearse backed up
making ruts through the grass.
The snow has a thin crust where it refroze.
It sounds different under your boots.
The tree, which had seemed
to *respire* somehow, to exude
a moist presence, is closed
up into itself, like a bone.
Your body's own heat
is a faith in things absent.

The sense of this landscape has changed.
Everything starts melting.
A dark bird alights on a branch.

I gave more than I thought I had.
I gave her stars that hadn't even been born.
I didn't know the price of what I gave.
I had been a secret from myself.
Part of the wind that shakes the trees.
Until she raised her eyes to mine. I took root.
Now the snow-covered tree seems painterly.
I feel it in myself, like a child
going back over letters or lines,
highlighting them with a different
color as he hums. As he sings.
In the quiet childhood living room.
At the old beach house. He sits back
to gauge the effect. Carefully erases.
I gave her gleaming gems
that dried into common stones. I learned
that words are empty sounds unless
someone agrees to understand them.
Love can never do justice
to another person. It's a mask you put on.
Everyone knows this.
On this rainy Tuesday, the clouds
are thick thoughts. Raindrops, icy,
sting my face. Fall into the land.
Punctuation marks in a vast Russian novel.

A splash of blood.
A drop of wine.
The earth drinks.
I step outside in an eager mood.
It's a task that needs doing.
There are people for whom it makes no sense.
So pretentious, they mutter.
I am sometimes one of those people.
I would try to explain it,
but my trying becomes
this thing
of twine, fog, bird skeletons. They
will not hear of such a thing. Won't see
this ground where anything can happen.
Imagine striking the tree with a stick.
Imagine a sound like a gong.
The sound goes on and on.
It frightens me.

A crow calls from the top of a pine.
If its cry were a spell,
the wind would start. Grow strong.
Pull the ground out from under me.
Fling me into the sky.
Why did I strike the tree like a gong?
The sentinel crow calls twice.
Another crow joins it. They flap off.
The grass is flocked with frost.
A derelict fountain glistens.
The sun climbs, blazing, through tangled trees.
Winter is passing from the world.
At its center, the light is ivory-citrus.
Stringent to peer at the way lemons taste.
Then orange-peach-crimson.
Then *ah*.

Few can hear
the one who sings out of sight.
Where no one's awake.
His crazy ambition.
His grief he was born.
Delight.
He's only a step or two
into the shadows,
trying his voice.
Before daybreak when the night is tall.
When massive shadows branch
into feathered silhouettes.
It's the art of being outrageous.
More often than not, the thing
that can't be true, that he's afraid
to say because
it can't be true, is true.
He has to sing it to find out.

His demons like the chalk-dry atmosphere
of classrooms, corridors,
where their knife-edged whispers
can feel like fact. They want him
stranded inside. Far from ponds. From clouds.
He senses them, ghostly fires sweeping through corridors.
It's good he has that stubborn
stone from the Eastern Shore on his desk.
The one that can ground his breath.
His mind is becoming
sunlight. The changing sky.

One wants that star he plucked from the river,
wet and glistening, when he was a child.
Won't accept that it's become a common rock.
The others want what they want.
Demon of silence. Demon of intellect.
Are they satisfied when he says, *I'm sorry I'm sorry?*
Does apologizing make them madder?
Some need a joke: They pop in a burst of laughter.
Or jaws get stuck. They glare around,
their jaws jammed open.
Some look like his father.
He knows they will come back
as they fold themselves away
into light. Except this one
who pleads with me. He wants
the gem I pulled from the river.

The secret to being beautiful.
Stop wanting beauty.
To be meaningful,
stop craving meaning.
Beauty and meaning are here.
Did you think you could add more?
The morning demands acknowledgment.
The sun is creating a salmon band
across the horizon.
The background traffic noise
has the texture of exposed concrete.
The dark bird sings: Its voice flags
then trills up higher than before.
You are there in the bird's throat.
You feel the force
of the song bursting through it.

He expects a noise but can't hear it.
His expectation is also a noise.
A dragon in his brain.
As soon as he hears it, he sees. He tastes
a harsh whiskey that lights him afire.
Sleeping dark angels open their eyes.
Let him pass. They dare not touch him.
Nothing seems to have changed.
Heaven to one side of the tree.
To one side of wherever he walks.
He hears halyards clang flatly against the flagpoles.
Not the ropes. The metal rings
that fasten the flags, rapping on metal.
Clanging and clanging.

Did someone bring the tree photo?
We stand in a circle around the tree.
Shapes around it shifting.
The tear-streaked child has brought the gleaming stone.
Hurry, he pleads. *Before it dries.*
The demon of silence would like to declare
that words are a sickness. A disease.
And you, he points out, *an ignorant man.*
Don't you know the world exists
apart from how you feel?
The seventh-grade teacher says, *Oh*
this is fabulous. Such a clever boy.
The giraffe agrees.
What was it we needed to say?
The original impulse?
The wise woman throws back her hood.
Reveals a crown of stars.
It was this, the child says,
setting the stone on the table.
We observe an awkward pause.
Someone else in the circle's speaking.
A voice made of rain.
The obsessive one
talks in a rapid monotone: *Take*
all the commas out put them back
take them out put them back.
The professor tamps his pipe:
This is much too clear.
The tragic one says, *Sometimes I feel*
like everyone dear to me died long ago.
What is that other person saying?
Can we get that down?
The naked woman says, *Oh that's good.*
Uh huh. I like that, too.
Oh baby oh baby!

Don't pretend you're blossoming if you're not.
However much you see blossoming
in others, don't believe it unless it happens to you.
The cemetery explodes with white.
If it's white, and it's blooming right now,
says a crotchety blogger,
it's a Bradford Pear and it's a disaster.
Never mind the tree's
weak structure, blown
apart after twenty years by any
half-hearted storm: It cross-
pollinates to produce
an earlier form of pear, the Chinese
Callery with 4-inch thorns.
Impenetrable thickets.
You walk that road among the trees—
You see happiness stopped in space.
Orion's belt. The Pleiades.
Blossoming.

Neither given nor received,
this love that exploded.
Later, they rose up
from the bed they had unmade.
To make sense of the debris.
How it flew apart then came
together. A Pasternak novel
falling into place. A modest
house on a busy street.
We didn't know what we were doing.
Their eyes rose to meet.
Here are the children still asleep.
He returns from his walk, to knock
on their doors. To say good morning.
A bird sings, *Teep. Teep teep.*
Buds on bare trees
swell up pointed with green.
The moon feels heavy.
Like Lara at her window.
Like her Yuri gone.

Trees that branch into slender dendrites,
almost touching, are not trees.
They are synapses in your brain.
Would you prefer to act cool?
Sneer at the flowers?
The world exists apart from how you feel,
but that apartness is a feeling.
Someone planted these blossomers
here for your enjoyment.
Each flower sits amid fine green sprays:
Like whiskers on a fish.
Take a few steps.
It should be easy
as a mouse's eyelashes.
Inhabit happiness.
Your happiness is so constructed,
you are always standing apart
and admiring it.
If you should find yourself in a high wind,
holding on for dear life,
do the prudent thing and let go.

Oh baby oh baby.
All winter you were covered
with fists clenched around nothing.
Staring down ice. Feeling ice.
You can't remember how or why.
You realized your fists held something.
You had to see what.
Last night, lightning flashed.
Thunder roared close by.
A crazy person inside you
was rearranging furniture, throwing
open windows, daring
rain to pour in.
Admit it. You wanted it.
The wind caught the storm door.
Flung it wide. Hinges screeched.
The door banged. And banged.
Wind comes rushing through the sunlight.
Trees leaning, swaying.
Grass quivers like millions of signal mirrors.
Blossoms are blowing from the pear trees, leaving them
in their scrawny green underclothes.
The petals collect on the side of the road.
No birds because of the wind.
The flags flap taut, metal rings
held apart from the flagpoles.
A crow scuds past, half
surfing the wind. The tree is blossoming.
Did you expect each bud to open
as a single flower? They open
like jewelry boxes, five or six
to a bud on slender stems,

each flower still tightly furled.
The blossoms are thick tassels,
plush brushes, cloth bells.
Purses widening to the bottom.
What is this feeling of great applause?
A metal ring clanging rapidly against a flagpole.
A crow calling as it flies out of sight.

The cherry gleams forth,
the shameless one.
Its tight red blossoms appear.
It gleams, a new name,
among plaques and stones.
Can you bear it?
To be that someone who looks east?
Toward nakedness?
Who walks into that fear?
An ordinary person?
Being extraordinary
means living in dread
of saying the wrong thing.
Of being dull. Out here,
there is no wrong,
no dull by the blossoming tree. Why
does each word have a side
you are blind to? A song
the best way to not know
what you're doing?
Abashed, walking into a sun
that rises beyond trees in the April cold.
Your eyes water. You look down
a little and to the left,
as if conversing shyly
with something unseen.

Why carry around this image of your father,
angry face floating in the sky,
radiating judgment, looking down on you?
In surprise, you touch that image of him.
It's thin like paper.
Go ahead. Lift a corner. Peel it away.
You were twelve and opened Aristotle.
The world shivered with silver.
Age twenty, school girls, chattering
in French on a speeding train:
For all you knew, laughing about Aristotle.
You want to open your mouth like they did.
Hear wheat fields tumble out. Or kindness.
Or the hum of bees. *Un arbre en fleur,*
one room over from understanding.
A foreign language. Crimson bells
burst into pink tutus. Parachutes
pop open. Skydivers suspended.
A new area of knowledge. Wounds
along the body. The revelations
of sex. Your own words
looking back: The familiar panic.
The image of your dad.

Robins have made a nest
of the pear blossoms, up by the roof
in the crook of the downspout.

Some days, it's best not to speak.
Thursdays. When the *tap tap* on a screen
gives way to a pause. Then *delete*.
Your whole brain, a wandering spotlight,
an eye in your forehead that doesn't blink.
The starlings discompose you.
The way they strut. The doves coo
in unison. Then rain: A change
in atmosphere. A metallic odor.
Fugitive splashes. Sidewalks spotting.
The cement transforms
from corrugated cream to gleaming gray.
Grass blades in a seam of asphalt flinch.

Beltane: In Celtic lore,
the beginning of summer.
Why must summer be
the unbroke stallion you can't ride?
You sense the veil between worlds.
So your dog goes for a walk.
That could be you holding the leash.
Afraid to stop because you might turn
into a stone, a stump, a tree.
The elf queen might ride by.
On her bay mare tinkling with bells.
She lures away those
who live from the neck up.
The feeling of Earth is strong.
The people buried here.
The rain taps on your coat in code.
The typing of telegrams
(*We regret to inform…*).
You can breathe,
let the world roll on. Or listen
for the bells of the queen.
Her hunting horn.

He balances between silence and speech.
Between hope that he
might talk his way
into friendship with the sky. And despair
that he's asking too much.
He's left with a choice of sentiment, that's all.
To be of consequence, to be that sinuous
voice in the dark, is to accept
defeat is possible.
The child never understood.
The crowd in love with lie after lie.
Admit this and still
because it's spring and the world
renews itself
walk down to that shore.
To the sighing tide.

He longs for the end.
The straight path. Turns.
Obeys the yoke of limit. Back
toward the children asleep.
His wife still in bed.
Unsure of the way.
Letting the dog guide him.
It's not really raining.
The air wants to be water.
Its liquid apostrophes shimmer.
The weather wants to be the tree.
The tree wants to be the weather.
He's mostly atmosphere.
Held together by longing. By light.
The path that once seemed straight
meanders. Demons
form ranks behind him,
daring him to look back.
The slow pounding, walking home,
as if leading the dead.
He thinks of his wife,
brushed by the sable
wing of cancer
that makes her living body
more precious. Its fading scar.
His daughter bursting with dreams.
His son.

It comes to this: I feel
I'm walking toward something true.
Something green I can taste,
like a sprig splitting,
that never belonged to words.
Beyond the gates
of boredom, doubt, grief,
lies the door to home.
To walk back through it and still
to work at kindness.
To see telephone wires, yard clippings.
Everything that was left out.
Trucks rumbling by
through intersections
of beauty and loss. Those branches
displaying leaves— saw-toothed.
Birds plummeting over fields.
The caretaker's pick-up,
its engine humming.
The man himself smokes a last
cigarette on his front porch.
Eyes me skeptically.
He lets me pass.

Sometimes I feel
like everyone dear to me
died long ago. Like you died too.
The spring, the tree as if aflame, the frantic birds.
I have survived myself. All I care about.
Mourned the death of everything.
Chugged that thick liquor.
My mind broods in a starless night,
dark bird, on an egg the size of a postage stamp.
I look into the egg, which is also
a tunnel, through which I see
everyone I care about.
Walking and talking. Feeling.
In a spring that once existed.
I tap tap at the egg.
Tap tap, it answers.

Start from that daily inarticulate shock.
Question your perfectionist streak.
Your fear of ridicule.
Good or bad, finished or not.
They can always ignore it if they want.
You don't have to know what it means.
The tree goes
from spiky and bare, bark
shiny and splotched, to thunderous
with leaves and back.
Birds alight. They fly away.

A man is looking inward at himself,
seeing the forest of the inarticulate.
Those tall pines.
His childhood was unremarkable. Why
does it tower that way above him?
Why, like it might explode?
Why desire, catching in his throat?
The bite of persimmon he can't cough up.
The old language of love. An underground
river beyond the roots of his tongue.
Why does anger say nothing?
He dreams of children, running
through the forest with sticks, who strike
the trees shouting, *Wake up, wake up.*

That image of your dad.

That's thin like paper.

Peel it away.

Dead twenty years,

he holds forth from his armchair.

By the picture window.

Mt. Saint Helens in the distance,

beyond the river,

its smooth white dome.

He's saying

something about the IRS. About the war.

At 12, you want to shine.

The way you sometimes do at school.

Extend his views, or disagree

a little, angling for approval.

The way his eyes

glare down at you.

Still.

Everyone in this house
is going crazy, my daughter says.
When I talk with you, you turn
the conversation.
With Mom, we end up with Bernie Sanders.
It's true we're all obsessed.
Her brother crouches before digital Pokémon.
He's written the ABCs of sheep.
Singing floats from my daughter's room.
Dad, she emerges to announce,
we're forming a band!
Ragged holes have been torn
in our walls by the plumber.
I stare through a gap in our bathroom
closet into the living room, feeling
the anatomy of this house.
My wife laughs over some
new post about Bernie Sanders.
Has anyone seen my Bernie T-shirts? She asks.
At the talent show, my daughter
walks to the front. Begins strumming.
Humans are weird, she starts singing,
Humans are queer.... From the alchemy
of her room, such tenderness.

Time for a good murder.
Attempting to hide the body.
For a love affair to go south.
A woman scatters strategic clues
in a monologue of local
color and misdirection.
The tree outside stands perfectly still
because no one could think of a breeze.
All the human stuff can now happen quickly.
Like in France, where everyone
stands much too close. Pages are filled
with grimaces and talk. In Sicily,
where an ancient blood feud reignites.
Or an obliging thunder shower
thunders, showers, while the hero
walks the streets, mourns human depravity,
frets at where the bodies have been hidden.
Rain down his face. T-shirt glued to torso.
Pages go by. The storm trundles off stage.
Put away in that drawer labeled, *Only*
for use in times of sadness or,
with dancing, to illustrate joy.
Open the door. A breeze is rising:
The leaves on the tree
flutter in the same direction.

Step out into the glowing.
The sun through the fog a fat pearl.
Water drops glisten from the tips of leaves.

You come to a gate of green.
Set like a frame in the earth. Overgrown
with honeysuckle. Alive with bees.
Don't let the news fool you. The world
is green. In most of it, most of the time,
nothing is happening. A tree
is standing where it always stood.
The sky beyond the clouds is in the midst
of its single continuous thought. The land
is full of what you've always felt.

At the green gate,
I'm an imaginary person.
Because the light is shining through me.
Leaves are growing where my heart was.

Remember trying to describe the world?
You only described yourself.
Like that woman once on the phone:
a lifetime of hurt in her *hello*.
Would you have thrown your words
out there so casually, if you'd remembered
the words were also throwing you?

I keep waking up,
my back to the wall.

A robin is saying, *Tcheus! Tcheus tcheus!*
Raw like a green sprig splitting.
He's *tcheusing* at you. You've stepped
out your door right next
to his nest on the downspout.
Sharp beak, tiny claws, as he swoops
from the wire. Hovers
a yard from your face.
For an instant, in your fear and his wings
against the sky, you see the messenger
of blood who cries, *This world
is no game, no dream you wander in.
Defend what you have.*

Some limbs are lopped off.
Fresh lemon ovals.
Exposed heartwood.
A professional job.
The caretaker must have thought
they encroached.
The limbs brushed
teasingly at his truck.
He anticipated the next storm.
How is a tree to know
when it's crossed the line?
How is a person?
This has happened a lot.
Branching out:
You see. You see. You see.
One day, your shadow
self shows up, a tool in hand.
With a smirk says, *Saw.*

A magician has snapped his fingers.
Everywhere you can hear
the sawing, taking
your world apart.
All night. All day.
Your head falls off even though
it's still on your shoulders.
The dog's rear end
starts out on its walk
as her snout returns.
Someone has sheered your wife's face
apart from her past. Her eyes,
her mouth, her skin, float free.
You don't know her again.
Each time she speaks she's a different person.
You can hear the sawing in your dreams,
vibrating in your chest, in time
with your breath. The world
is drifting apart into islands,
painfully clear,
surrounded with steam.
Someone is sawing the world
into planks. Piling them in the heat
into stacks of a hundred boards each.

Yes, he's a subject of interest.
File thick as a novel.
You have to think like these perps.
By self report, he's 5-foot-ten.
Measures 5-foot-nine.
Write this in your notebook it's important.
There's been a mid-life cringing of his spine.
He's indifferent to his appearance.
He's left collars and cuffs
and button-downs far behind.
His tee's, which come untucked,
his jeans, inching down
until he has to jerk them up, are spotted
with stains from eating
in front of screens.
His glasses have accumulated dust.
His ears aren't clean.
He combs with his fingers.
His hair is easily startled.
He mutters, or stops to tap
at his phone. Or lifts it up
as if in worship to a tree.
We have a team at work
to account for these behaviors.
Why? you ask. This mystery
has stymied our investigators.
We've looked at transcripts of his therapy.
That doctor. Cruelly
assuring him he's normal. Thus
removing his last conceit: he might
be someone's interesting monster.
A white chalk aura

starts to materialize
about him, an outline around his body.
An interesting trick—if a breach
of procedure—the way he manages
to be dead, skipping the part
where he dies.

Your father in his armchair.
Behind him, his world
of golf courses and highways.
It's a shock to remember him
driving, sharing jokes with his friends.
Apart from your ideas about him.
Those things he may have said, or looks
he cast, that made the breath catch,
the heart stammer, are not
gone exactly. He was more.
Reading the newspaper. Getting in
another nine holes before dark.

See him pacing the floor.
Standing apart.
Alone in his worries.
It hits you that success was not certain.
The surprise is, you made it. All
his children. Even you.
Can't you give him that?
He worked? He tried?

But the war.
Your older brother's number
approaching like a match
toward dynamite.
Then the dangers
drifting away: His flight
to Canada. Other
possible misfortunes.
Your mother's saints protected you.

Remember
how it was *building building building*.
Tufts of green stuff in between.
Driving driving.
Chanting as you drove:
What you had to be when?
Who you had to be how?
Stepping out each day,
into Nature, in your pajamas, to admire
the mockingbirds, the chirping robins. How they
flew past you and away? The theory was
to walk triumphantly until a robin
screamed at you. Looked you in the eye.
Its beaky glare pushed back to madness.

It was a green world on which the buildings stood.
It was rolling rolling hills through which
a road cut. An invisible
stream among bushes.
Trees reaching up. Wind blowing. Then
a sky river, flowing. Bearing
the green world and its buildings
along. Someone had to say,
Go baby you go be.
She had to say, *Look wind, here*
is your space to roam in. Tree,
your sky to fill with leaves. Creating us
must have been nothing compared
with letting us go. So the sun is released
to climb the sky. You regret
the times you turn away.

Now being a father yourself:
Until you understand him,
his anger will burst through you.
You are not men, either one,
who thought of escape.
You were trapped by this life.
You put down roots.
It was the trap you wanted.
You were playing the long game.
Choosing to be vulnerable.
To stop dreaming of another world.
To make your stand in this one.
To love it with the love you had,
imperfect as you were. To marry
another person who could hurt you.
Worse, whom you could hurt. To open
up to the almost unbearable
love for your children, unable
to predict what the world
would throw at them, what they
would throw back.
This common story:
To work, to try. To watch it all
culminate in leafy stillness.

When you walk again
among people, you are maybe
80-percent forest.
When you look into their eyes, the sun
is casting a shadow as it rises.
When conflict comes,
you no longer have that feeling
of being elbowed out of existence.
Because you stand, not in yourself
but in Baltimore, the shove,
when it arrives, is against the rain—
or against unyielding
funereal stone. So what
if they shoulder you out of the way?
They can't stop the pouring down.
The circling birds growing louder.
If you have chanted, chanted, until
you are kneeling on the ground,
your voice will be filled with the cries
of birds. With everything that's real.
Those others will have no answer but
to reveal themselves. That is the theory.

The day we got married,
the preacher forgot about us.
He had to be tracked down
at a Chinese restaurant in Pennsylvania.
No one was sure how to cut the cake.
The temperature in the courtyard, a hundred degrees.
Your uncle, who taped the ceremony,
kept veering the camera
back to the attractive harpist.
We departed to cheers, waving
from my sister's cherry-red Citröen.
The top open, standing.
Our marriage that day was mostly sky,
with the tops of a few trees.
No minor impediments could stop us,
in our wedding clothes made of clouds
and light. You imagined endless days,
companionably, by the sea.
I could hardly believe my luck, joined
forever with my best friend.
Over time, the world grew up
into that picture: branches, trunk,
the roots, the entire tree.
The shape of the land.
Oh my dear sweet peach.
You've learned how I
can trudge along. I've learned
how your shadow self can gleam,
knocking over furniture,
looking for ways to escape.
Our marriage includes
everything falling apart.

The tree being bare.
Then thrusting out leaves.
The sky is bright. Behind it,
as behind a screen,
someone is frying an egg.
Installing a shower curtain.
Laughing or talking too loud.
Our marriage includes
power lines strung everywhere.
Dogs barking in smoldering yards.

The fragrant smoke of human kindness.
More than anyone can deserve.
This human queerness.
To live with its discomfort.
I can't bless myself. My words
are empty sounds unless
someone agrees to understand them.
I want to be near my friends.
I want their touch.
To look into their faces.
I'm lonely for my wife.
Being part of a family.
Released, by a word, a glance,
from shame and fear.
From work, she sends me a text:
How's your morning? What are you doing?
I'm making breakfast.
Counting the years.
I'm lonely for our children who are still asleep.
I think I walk out past the tree,
through the heat and the buzzing cicadas,
only to measure how lonely I feel.
If I can look on this world
and not be moved, at least I can notice
the being-shaped hole
where I could have been.
If I can't love any more,
I can contemplate the love-shaped absence.
If I walk to the far edge of the cemetery,
through a gap in the fence, down
a steep trail, I know I will come
to a stream in the woods—glass sheets sliding
over massive faces of stone.
This tree beside me, the ridge
outlined in light.

Your street at the city edge:
Brick duplexes, bungalows,
rigged up at the end of a war.
Men putter in their yards, half
astonished that time exists.
Nature is not really Nature—more
like weeds out of control—that someone
meant to get around to.
And one day they are trees.
Think of the Ancients: The journey
to anywhere, long and tedious.
If you stood in a field and wanted music,
you had to sing. Go back far enough,
you had to invent Song.
The gods would come for dinner.
Now comes the long music
of tires humming to the road.
The rolling green on either side like a wake.
Call it *vacation* or a *family reunion*.
You asked for yards and were given
these miles unspooling under your feet.
To Georgia: slotting another
nozzle into the tank. You lean
against the car in the midst
of a sudden shower. How
did the world become so large? Its clouds
rumbling up ahead.
Being part of a family.
Gathering in the hills.
The cicadas around us singing. Everyone
seated at the long table
as if a light shines on them.

The noble gases, the metals, the nonmetals
jostle for position.
You're one of the elements.
You laugh, argue, wave to each other
from opposite ends of the table.
While on TV, half noticed,
politicians and pundits buzz.
It's awkward, when you're an element,
what you say to another element.
You just want to look at them.
Brothers and sisters, mother,
nieces, nephews. Drink in
whatever is in their faces.
Something familiar that strengthens you.
Of which you're a part.
The dead are here also.
Grandmothers and -fathers,
amongst you, drinking you in.
Do you want to talk?
Discuss what you want. You are
related more deeply than words. Even
than like or dislike. Anything
they can say will feed your hunger.
Something simple attaches you.
Not personalities or politics.
You're not in that dusty box.
This one endures like iron. This other
like oxygen lights up a room. Maybe
this third one has properties
that are yet to be discovered.
A primal face, multiplied and refracted.
You read these words
aloud at the long table. There
is the demon of silence amongst them.

The silence around your father.
The way his words
elbowed other words
aside. When he shouted at you
from across the dinner table.
Communist!
The worst word he knew.
Years later, you saw
a picture of Mt. St. Helens
erupting in the *New York Times*.
Outside the hotel where you worked
near Central Park. You were looking
at the papers stacked for sale.
Each picture full of smoke.
Ash blanketed your parents' yard.
The mountain's dome
became a crater's crown.
A brother reminds you, *You
were the only one
who talked back, out of all of us.
Who challenged him.*
You say, *Yeah,
I was just that stubborn.*
Another brother says,
*We turned out okay. He must
have done something right.*
Driving home, you feel
the panic approaching. You stop
the car at the side of the road.
Heart beating fast, you think
you're going to die.
Your wife, your children, looking on.
You can't get air.

Cicadas peer through compound eyes,
encumbered by cloudy wings.
The *imagos*, males preponderantly,
are nearly hollow, gutless wonders,
existing only to call and call.
They emerge in fierce July.
The females cut slits in twigs to deposit eggs.
Soon nymphs will hatch. Drop.
Burrow back into the soil. Sleep
until the heat, again,
wakes them to an angry panic.
That segmented life span
explains why they never
learn anything.
Not knowing their own story,
they cannot hear themselves.
Their voices begin
as a kind of drumming.
Slowed down, they resemble
drums of war. Speed them up,
a clicking. Then the alien
familiar buzzing from everywhere.
Gutlessness becomes an amplifier:
Its hollowness makes it loud.
The cicada sings of rugged
individualism without the individual.
Even by itself, a chorus. Unlike
the cricket, which it superficially resembles,
stridulating in the distance.
A lone violinist. On acid.

Not enough wind to budge the leaves.
The cicadas ratcheting up.
Their rattle, electricity arcing,
the noise that leaks from damage,
builds to a maddening buzz.
Stops. Starts again.
Crickets, their music not unlike
the shaking of sleigh bells,
express the satisfaction the world feels
at being destined for fire.
A vast sun rises. The world
is riding a mad crow into flame.
The cicadas' whir, louder and higher,
will be the sound of incineration.
Branches will thin
out as the light
eats them away. What
is the source of kindness?
Last night, the dreams came
filled with the ringing of crickets.
The winter to come, singing.

I peel away images of my dad.
Until he's half imagined.
World War II has ended.
I can't believe Dad is so young.
I imagine him in the dark, talking
hesitantly about the future.
How the dark
turns Mom's eyes
into faint gleams looking back.
Her body next to his.
They didn't know what they were doing.

We humans are queer.
Furless, laughing. Half animal, half thought.
It's outrageous we're here.
Eating a burger. Drinking our beer.
A queer light shines on us like we've
been photo-shopped. We wander
in two dimensions. Flat.
Change the world by stepping into it.
Postpone our nakedness:
attribute it to others. Dance
in circles we call *religion*.
Tell queer and crazy stories:
Imagine a god, thrust in the ground,
sprouting again.
Or we're damned. We're lost.
We flinch at those unlike us because
we are so unlike ourselves.
Among us, a rare saint
will live with the discomfort
of his human queerness.
Will speak an outrageous truth because
she knows of nothing
more outrageous than being here.
Will step into the Wild, and it stays wild.
Not blaming another
for what cannot be helped.

In August, he discovers
his affinity for winter. He loved
to lean his mind into the land.
Everything visible. Houses. Crests of hills.
His thoughts were clear.
He stood at the gates of myth and symbol.
He rests his head against his wife's shoulder.
Oh my dear. The summer is too mighty.
The sun, a trumpet, blasts open their front door.
The fox and the peacock appear at the head of an army.
In August, he wakes to this panic:
What does it mean to speak
his dreams? To rest his thoughts on the quiet
shrubs and grass in a cemetery.
Queen Anne's lace, balanced
on tall stems beside a road. He comes back
to the tree, growing by itself, rooted
in vulnerability. Returns
to its innocence like to a well.
Hears grass grow. Each leaf of it
a *yawp* shorn off at the top.
A cry that longs to cover the earth.
Wants the earth to be a lawn. The lawn,
a meadow, a plain. The grass, a nation.
Each spear, a Napoleon bent on world domination.
Horizontally, it gets as far as the road.
Vertically, it gets mowed.
He wakes to this panic, that words mean nothing.
Sits on the edge of his bed, aware of his breathing.

The thought that what you say might be true
can make it untrue.
It's fortunate, now and then,
when you forget to lie.
There's a helpless feeling. You try
everything and fail. You examine
how emotions come out of words.

The demon of silence urges, *Learn
how to tune an engine. Take
a second job. Or a third. It's never
too late to study business, to really
carefully mow the lawn.*

Now the words have grown quiet.
They sit in your mouth. Unspoken, metallic.
You sense your saliva. Swallow
blackberries straight from the branch,
pulling them down to your tongue.
You can taste them.

It's a day for noticing: The fine hair
on your skin. The places where you ache:
Your feet, your hips. The left side
of your face, with age, has become less mobile.
You're staring out of one eye with surprise.
You swing out of bed. Find your balance. Breathe.
The light of this day fills the room.
Your spouse in bed still asleep.
The silence bright. The rasp of crickets. And you
are a middle-aged bear, who lumbers
from its cave on hind feet, toward the tree,
the fountain, toward cricket song, the doleful
crow cry. Somewhere out here there is honey.

It is time to give up. Open your eyes.
Summer is a vacant house. Beyond it,
bulldozers rumble. So easy
for everything to go. The sky to crack.
To wait for the first light that will never show.
A squirrel moves by leaps to the nearest trunk.
A deer gives you a look.
The reason for the deer is gone.
Something should be said. No one's saying it.
Something inexplicable must be explained.
People let go of dreams.

The landscape drifts closer to what it was.
The leaves still cling.
A fat cloud hugs the horizon.
Above it, cirrus wisps, tinged pink.
The lawn, in green and straw, is dotted with graves.
The crickets sing. Through them, you hear
a foreground, a background, stained by sound.
A few leaves waver. A few
have turned brown.
At the end of the world, the fountain spouts—

Trees. Houses. The outline of a city.
Hills. The harbor. Clouds.
Go back far enough, the background
stops changing. If it did change,
it would do it slowly,
a deep color deepening. Cloud rivers,
motionless until you see them
flowing. A pristine leaf showing a fleck.
The memory of towers falling: People
leaping from the fire, suspended
more than fifty floors up. Till the background
is still wherever you go.

The moon follows you as you drive.
Rows of trees accelerate between you.
Even when you're in a crowd, even at a party.
The moon is nailed to the sky.
You try to say the color of what's colorless.
How stillness moves. How silence
is a sound, a roar. How your time here
goes by like the tolling of a bell
in a place where no bell has rung before.

A slow walk past the tree each morning
leaves a residue like smoke—
that stays with you all day, flows
at night into your dreams.
The grass, the trees, the clouds,
are a cloak you can wear
nonchalantly like a medieval squire.
It's a good look on you.
The chirp of insects makes a strong soft wool.
The felt of what was felt.
The turning leaves are brown threads.

The cloak is also made
of driving those twisty roads to work.
Hills speeding down to traffic lights.
The urgent feel of disc brakes.
Take the fork upwards, shift gears,
round the corner while the trees
beside the road, the sky above the trees,
all shimmer. Then you're sitting
at your desk, in a cubicle, typing,
talking on a phone, the sun
shining through plate glass.
The day inside you still moving
relentlessly forward.
As if you're still driving.
Still talking to Dusty.

I can't tell if this world is real.
If imagined, it isn't me imagining it.
It was done. Even if no one did it.
The tree was *tree'd*. The sky
was *sky'd*. The world was *worlded*.
It's still being *worlded*. Every second.
The tree brought back to stand at the same spot.
There, between a thought
and stone where the thought is stopped—or air
where the thought expects to stop
but can't: The dragon lives.
Moving when everything is still.
Too big to be heard.

Dry leaves scatter, scatter, scatter.
Rain falls. All day. Into night.
Pauses. Falls again. Falls. Then falls.
The air becomes cool. Like something
a deer would nibble
shyly. The grass is soaked. No sunrise yet.
A blush in the clouds
farther south than expected.

The leaves were terra cotta for days.
Or bright yellow. Now:
Venetian red, deep brown, pale gold.
With black and rust blemishes,
folded and battered. They macerate in puddles.
Form shaky lines where the grass stops.
The pavement is stained wet an extra foot around them.
A shape swims beneath
while the clouds thin. There's this ambient glow.
Dimly, the moon: three quarters full.

A third tower is still burning.
The light along the horizon
is a drop of vanilla in milk.
Years have gone by.
Some people might still be saved.
Open your eyes.
It seemed impossible a landscape
should still exist around you.
All landscapes were folded up, put away
that day. All clouds with their colors
from peach to purple, smudges
of smoke and plum. Then life
went on. It was
an awakening to catastrophe.
The tree gave up its perfect stillness.

Now geese fly down to the pond.
And stories don't work anymore.
The hero's journey, the death of the old man,
the lovers married. You know
how they end: happily and sadly.
People cry because
their lives are out of stories.
They should be glad.
Of that black sky.
In front of it, blacker trees.

In the un-storied world,
it's raining steadily. Empty
but still too full. Too many
details jammed together. Too many
cars for the narrow streets.

An accident up ahead. You're stopped
in traffic—horns and a vibration
of engines—giving up
the urgency to get somewhere.
The on-ramp to the story is blocked.
Rain drums the roof of your car.
Water slops down the side of a bus.
A woman sings on the radio:
Billy Ray was a preacher's son.

The world begins to chime.

The tree speaks.

You sprout training wings.

Burst into flame.

Walk around, careful

not to harm anybody.

No one notices you're on fire.

Out of a crowd,

one dusky flower

turns toward you. Reality

quavers about its axis, returns

a tree to the same spot.

A sky to its blue.

That ultramarine in Giotto.

With a few stars.

She is that beautiful.

The horizon is waiting.

Light the color of parchment

comes up steadily from below.

The whole east, lit by a single candle.

Great blocks of cloud clearing the sky.

There's a single crow. You can hear it.

You are famous already.
You always were, even
when no one knew you.
The way a tree can star
in its own opera. That first
colossal leaf tumbling
to earth. A blade of grass
is a best seller. You desired
your name in other mouths.
Your image licked by other
eyes like a flame. You thought
you desired. When the book
fell open. When you looked
at those words, greedy
for them to be yours.
There was nowhere else to go.
You wandered so long,
trying to find what you are.

It's time to give up
trying to please your mother.
Or your weird aunt.
Or Miss Frank, your seventh-grade teacher.
Your college instructor. To give up
pleasing your father, as if
you knew how. He's passed beyond
approving or disapproving.
That uncle who seemed to know stuff
but wouldn't tell. Give up. He's gone.
Don't make things worse
calling him back. Some people
will only turn away harder.
Praise from others
is a gale you have to withstand because
you want it so badly.
While most of the world
settles into indifference.
Time to give up
trying to sway it toward you.
The way the tree is indifferent.
The way the dead are. Stay
on your feet.
Listen to yourself.
Barking like a seal.

The doors of summer have been pushed shut.
Massive, blackened by flame.
The tall figure shutting them
is a god we know. A heavy angel.
He has the strength of grief.
The awareness of death.
But no name. Maybe
he's just a shadow. Putting
one hand on each door.
Leaning his weight against them.

Because of this god, the world continues,
its rivers of fallen leaves along the road,
its wind-lashed sky. October
enters the air
the way dreams unspool.
The warm days falter.
Layers of fog recall
how to arrange themselves.
The body, how to gnaw on grief.
Autumn is a slow-
moving problem of organization:
There's a summer to disassemble,
a wind to blow things bare.
Against expectation, most leaves,
still green, cling to their branches.
A few flush red like flames underwater.

Passions that never had much
to do with calendars
rise out of bones. Out of roots.
Halfway in and out of songs.
Emotions you forgot to feel.
At the depth of the exhale: a knot of tears.
It could be all the grief there is.
Getting up each day is the best you can do.
Stare when spoken to.
As the narrowing
light between the doors
flares more brightly.

Clouds that migrate overhead: full
of the consciousness of whales.

If the necks of geese were a story,
no one would believe how far they extend ahead of their wings.
How the wings ripple like water.
Or rain on my upturned face,
full of everything I did wrong in my twenties.
No one would believe it's all been gathering.
When every emotion came out
too fast for me to stop it. Someone cried.
When I froze, in a panic, feeling
what I didn't want to feel. I could never
imagine past summer, that blunt green.
I'm glad what I've done comes back,
and I drink it. My life in a cup.
The liquor of it. Rain of it.
No one can drink it for me.
I welcome the wind, the cold,
the bare branches to come.

More crows gather.
They hover, so many tattered kites.
A leaf makes a soft *tick* on landing
to check off its own task.
The wind starts.
Other leaves set sail.
First a few, then thousands.
Tumble up the street and over
the horizon, clattering till the trees are bare.
Clouds slide hurriedly in the same direction.
Scrape the sky till it's all that same blue.
The wind blows harder:
Trash cans tip over, rumble loudly up the road.
Old trees, starting to fall, set off car alarms.
The wind picks people up mid-sentence:
Weather reporters, TV pundits,
undecided voters, candidates for office.
Tumbles them end over end out of sight.
They look so surprised: to be light like leaves.
People on their way to work,
first a few then thousands.
Still waving their arms and legs.
They hold desperately onto lamp posts
and car door handles. Their feet
bicycle in the sky. Their hands let go.
The wind blows harder. *Harder.*
Grabs words out of people's mouths.
Harder. Off radio transmission towers.
Out of books till the pages are blank.
Harder. All the font styles end over end.
Briefly catching on telephone wires.
Blowing the books away. Blowing

away houses. Away trees, hedges.
Everything clattering till the world is bare.
That blue sky. That green horizon.
That wind blowing even harder.
Till the ground lifts up in great curtains of sod.
The blue peels off, streams away in ribbons.
The glow behind everything like a candle.
Someone sitting in that light, reading
my palm.

The pundits continue to talk.
It's their job.
To get things wrong
in predictable ways.
Part of me
will not move on through this gate.
Will stay motionless
before the television.
Too radiant to pass through.
Will sit on the sofa. Lie on it.
Will always feel the trap door
at the bottom of the mind
swing open.
Will never be ready
to breathe in
the sharp cleansing stink
(while the rest of me keeps breathing, must
keep breathing) rising
out of the unfinished
basement. Below
the hurricane door
kept decorously shut.
Just keep breathing, *mon vieux*.
Keep breathing as the dog
licks your face.

The world empties of everything
but yes or no. Any gods
you've not met personally must go.
You must decide who is your friend.
Forget the incidentals:
Leaf. Crow. Who lied.
Here in this place of fathers and feathers.
Whether things matter when leaves are gone.
When you look through trees into the land.
At how the sky looks. How the sense
of the landscape has changed.
Into long hill-lines, summer-hid houses.
The dark bird perched on a branch.
The shards of the leaves still swirling.
The blank world looking back.
I think it has always been looking.
Even when you yell—or groan with love—
a part of you is this land, this sky.
Bare twig ends trembling. The same
trembling that's in your blood.
That's in each quill.

The autumn complexion of your face
when you look at me.
When I'm holding you in our bed, caressing
your forked branches, your leaves,
When you straddle me from above,
our gazes coming near.
A father, a mother, after years of familiarity.
You look past the many faces I put on.
You're just yourself. You're also more.
Each morning you're the sky
sitting across from me at breakfast.
I rush through doors to get inside,
to get to you, only to find myself
back in the rain. Or early, in the cold,
among fading stars.
It's your look I sense, peeling me
back to a simple figure on the land:
The stronger my feeling, the calmer the calm.
Till it settles into a fierce quiet.
My face in the cold a stinging mask.
A part of me that is curious, that waits for you
to go so I can see what happens next.
To measure how much love there was. Know.
A part of me that waits to go, too. To know what's left.
This winter land that sees down all the roads.

Only to find myself
out in the fog, which is not fog.
Which is trees just having
forgotten what makes them real.
Some days in December,
they're abstract like numbers, dissolved.
Thinning as the mist encroaches, eats them away.
They join the company of unreal things.
Back off to where the world ends
fifty feet from here. Except
this tree, this one, too close, too heavy
with now. And now. A cello's long-held tone
leaning into space.

I imagine my father as a boy.
I love him like that.
The prospect of me
not even dust, not even
a scrap of paper swept up behind him.
Startled sheep part ahead of him;
flocks of rock doves burst apart
as he gallops to reach home
before dark on Bonnie Bell his pony.
I keep peeling scenes away
till I realize with surprise:
I've broken through. A faint
breeze blooms against me from the other side.
I look out into the endless spirit of my dad.
Imagine his eyes somewhere
in the star-filled dark, looking back at me.
The look I never saw when he was alive.

SAM SCHMIDT is also the author of *Suburban Myths* (BEOTHUK BOOKS, 2012). For more than a decade he edited and published *WordHouse*, a newsletter for Maryland writers, and hosted the reading series WordHouse at the Minás Gallery. He is a two-time recipient of the Maryland State Individual Artist Grant and has a Master's Degree in Comparative Literature from the Johns Hopkins University. Schmidt lives and works in Baltimore, Maryland.

www.ingramcontent.com/pod-product-compliance
Lightning Source LLC
Chambersburg PA
CBHW032053290426
44110CB00012B/1074